closer baby closer

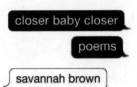

closer baby closer

poems

savannah brown

For E. We tried!

Contents

1.

2.

3.

My body is a cage that keeps me from dancing with the one I love, but my mind holds the key.

Arcade Fire

It is in your self-interest to find a way to be very tender.

Jenny Holzer

1.

Because the bird flew before there was a word for flight,
years from now there will be a name
for what you and I are doing.

Marcelo Hernandez Castillo

Pain theory

The story of the masochist's daughter
only ever had one ending. Under the nail
skin unravels like a secret
orange peel. A blood blister
yawns awake on her trigger finger.
She learns to lucid dream so she can die
and not die. She is not afraid of knives
or bad news. Not the plane crash. Not putrid
water fear-chopped through the throat.
Pain is the answer to a question
her life is gathering the words to ask.

The punchline is that when she grows up
she becomes a lover, an acrobat who each perverted
sunrise jumps from an unsurvivable height
certain she can talk some sense into the fall.
There's a line between pain and pleasure
as much as there's a line between two eternities
and anyway, this could be worse. The air
is giving you one billion breathless kisses,
lover. The ground wants you.

Sudden fall long stop

You're kissed
in orange light and I'm painting
the gazebo with all the wine I've spilt,

drunk off my tits. I am queen of neon
winter. I am not in love! Hooray! London
heaps metal oceans over ant hills, calls it wonder

and we're here to disgrace it together,
paid for tickets,
but the mind tends to travel alone,

now you're not just orange under the heat lamp,
it is very important that ~you~ are *orange*
under this ({hEaT lAmP})!

Exclamation points jive
round your warm little face and I notice
you could ruin my life.

Because of the sort of person I am
I want to drag you onto the drop tower
but you're afraid of heights

and the weightless sensation of falling
you get from the float

of your organs,
or at least their strange upward tug,
including the heart,
yes maybe yes especially the heart,

this moment rings in me like loose change
that all lands head-side,
oh no,

it's true. Once you're up there, I mean.
The only way back is down.

Sex poem

Just to think of her holding me down
tugs up the telephone wire stitched with every species
of flying bird
by a synchronous exhilaration
of wings
There will be no more calls today
No more electric crumbs pinging
pointlessly from place to place
I'm talking about something bigger
A fevered displacement
of air
A star unseamed to tease
out a parade of smaller stars
All the soil in one motion turned
wet side

Recorded talismans of intimacy

One million hairs left on the carpet in the event you need to clone
me

Contacts left to wilt on the bathroom counter
    (cerulean half-globes, shed skin)

Tits in alleyway at rose-colored dusk

A missed call that dangles from a thread in space like a baby tooth

Stalagmites of night shell crusted to waterline

Thong discarded cloudy side

The desire to hear about your day relentless as a fetish

Ornaments of razor burn

A word mispronounced and swiftly mocked

Funnel of breath on a bleached scalp

Scrambled! Eggs! For You! Again!

A decade-old robe round daybreak body
iced and sexed

Where the childhood home's head had been there is a blossoming

In this infinite Venn diagram I'll meet you in the middle

The part of the statue everyone touches
for luck

A little orb made of our liquefied fates

A stargate lodged in the rib

My baby my baby

I will know you well enough
to find you again
in the place where none of this is

The problem with other people

is that one must leave before the other
+ one always gets there first. Words
left in my notes app when I was too eager
and soon: *hoax, lonely drum, I'm
only typing this to look wanted,*
but you + I once discovered
we had arrived on opposite ends
of the same damned train, and when
the day became a grey-blue smolder
but appetite still flashed its barb
one of us said, well, why can't we
just stay? + how obvious it felt to stay,
our common history as new and bright
as a bulb. This is the decision, to know
you and keep knowing—our forms framed
in the yellow second story window
like displaced moons who've found
the other in the same foreign orbit,
who meet + continue to meet
even after all the easy words have gone.

Unmute me unmute me unmute me!

Haven't you heard
that if the weakness stays

in the throat it doesn't exist? O
to be as stupid and bold as an alarm

programmed to wail *hold me*, or grisly
city foxes whose fucking sounds like female death.

Don't let the capitalists
fool you: to want is to be humiliated,

and love
takes you two-thirds of the way through grovel.

He's bored of the silence we're gummed
in, I know. He blinks from across the table.

His eyelashes look like many small roads
to nowhere.

Someday with my pointer finger
fish-hooked down my throat

I'll hoist out the cotton like a boy from a well
who knows everyone's secrets.

I have so much practice now breathing,
which from a distance looks like

I'm finally deciding to ask for what I need,
but at the last moment changing my mind.

What you realize after the fight

To love is to reveal
the pale underbelly of the
arm or to fashion
from the magnifying lens
a prism it is to dilate
oh god dilate or to turn
your splintered rib
death side down against
the gauze or to come if
baby says come and should
baby say I need you to try
and come closer than that
you surrender your callus
your swan cracks with song
oh to love is to open
your mouth very wide—

Poet (derogatory)

He likes my poems because 'it's interesting to see
how differently we experience the same moment'
which was a nice way to say I'm always overreacting.
Meanwhile I hate poems and myself for writing them,
these monologues delivered in riddle by a troll
who guards the bridge to a place no one even wants
to go, like hell, or an open mic, where a further
coalition of trolls guard further bridges.
I try so hard.
Spend hours on the word *tongue,* a comma.
Look at this experimental maze intended
for an animal both winged
and extinct. And don't get me started
on love; my term of endearment, today I tried
to tell you you're the chosen one in a long-dead
language, wrote an instruction manual for disabling
an atom bomb in cipher, blasted slow-growing peonies
into space to move them closer to the sun.
Why can't I just say it straight?
I'm so in love with you it makes me want to die.
Understand.
Anyway, we know words always win. I'm sorry,
another lie. Sometimes they win but often
they lose. This is the truth: I have nothing else.

First date

Picked a cute pub, at least,
Friday night, Hoxton strip,
twinkly and wood-panelled,
good vibes.
Two still unadjusted
to the other's way of being.
Silences. Uncertain chitters.
Watching them is a little painful.
They cover their mouths
when they chew or they laugh.
Their knees
are a practical epoch apart.
So unlike how I know you:
like being given regular
transfusions of my own dirty
blood, watching the sun rise
over a world I invented, one
I'm so afraid to begin again.

Notes on your dramatic exit from the house party

you leave behind

    a distant toll of group laughter at a joke you didn't hear

    + balmy home air from someone else's childhood

    + a gin-sticky monologue from someone almost you but worse

    + everyone's hands tessellated on lover's chest
                yours does not fit

    + the black yolk of night slinking down your neck

    + plushy leg fat straining against a grater
            of fishnet

    + incredibly important little baggies

    + the reflective rain-washed nowhere street

    + your ticket home

    + the apparent but inaccessible tomorrow in which you feel better

    + the dark shrinking room

+ the social fallout
+ the hole at the end of it

if a part of the world was made for you it is not here
you have never been further from love cut in your shape

look! there's a plane carving chemtrails in the night and they say

IN PURSUIT OF EXTREME MODERNITY
YOU HAVE BECOME INSUFFERABLE

CONGRATULATIONS YOU ARE SO DRUNK
AND SO CONTEMPORARY AND WITHOUT A CLUE

OH YOU DO LOVE THEM   YOU DO   JUST NOT
IN THE WAY THAT LETS BOTH OF YOU LIVE

New year's, overstimulation

each time Juliet dies her lips
are warm and blue with juice that precious little
bitch. could she have wanted harder / I'm told
my questions ruin otherwise pleasant
afternoons / anyway, wounds. the one in the car park
that still flexes as if swallowing. one in the backyard,
nightflayed. when I'm upset the sun becomes
a scab and was always a scab. another in the alley
that gagged on the past and kept gagging.
possession can mean that something is yours
or that something is living inside you.
cherry wound wants to be filled, apologizes
for its glint. each bad day's a reverse conch shell,
they're sucking the sound of the sea out of me,
a worm with my face rolls around on the bed sheet,
says if I wasn't put on the planet to worry, then God,
look at all this wasted time.

Retroactive jealousy

Like a perfectly black rectangle hovering π
inches above the highway

it's harrowing
but vague enough to deal with later

like cosmic desynchronization

and not the sort of nice kind like being
jet-lagged or day drunk

more like the cultural rancidness I feel
while watching my friends
silently watch commercials

like an epidemic of suicidal moths

bashing out their brains against
the city strip neon reading *girls girls girls*

like the recurrent UTI
of the mind

When baby fingers
my mascara from under my eyes my whole
face comes off in baby's hands

Obsession grants me the precision
of a surgeon who operates
only on incredibly hot girls

They show up bearing tasteful hand
jewellery and razor-sharp
banter and really decent music taste

pussy brain-pink, back arched

as a cat about to be sick

a giggle like a little bell rung
by pheromones wearing sleepover pajamas

lips which never touch
lest she conceal her sweet half-wafer of teeth

like in my mind she even has the sexiest knees
I've ever seen

petal skin, wine stain red like a watercolor
brush bleeding into spring water

Girl knees! This is what I've become

rationality croaks

the suicidal moths
have risen from the dead
and are now circling the source
of the dark.......negamoths

Being smart has nothing to do with being smart
I look at you and lose language

Someday I'll care for something
without wanting to close a door behind it

Sorry

New love has made me completely
insane. At lunch an old friend asks
insanely good? and I say no, insane.
Fearing betrayal makes me seem
important and kingly, like someone worth
assassinating. Every time a skeptic
has prophetic dreams a book
is unwritten, science undiscovers
a crucial equation, a star winks back
into black nothing.
Think of a sound so loud
that it wakes up everyone on the planet
except the sound is only the thwack
of your heart. Sweetie. You're the only one
here. All I want is to be told
that something that hasn't happened yet
was always going to happen
and there was nothing I could do.
Once I lumbered to the kitchen
ready to be difficult and mean
I burnt myself on hour-old tea.

I kept remaking it so when you came down
it would be warm. Oh you perfect

idiot. I bet you did. Nothing gentler has ever happened.

When I'm better I'll find what went missing,

the books, the equations, the stars,

and give them straight to the boy in the kitchen

that day, they're for him, have it all.

Olbers' paradox

Instead of the moth-nibbled tarp that flaps
soundly now above us, instead of all this faint
topography and solar grit, the astronomers say

the sky should bare a superdense sheet
of stars, to hell with constellations, the night
watched only by one devastatingly bright eye.

Let it be known I'm glad it's not true.
It would be too much and too beautiful. Nothing
would get done. We would overextend our necks
and spend all the dark hours weeping. It would be like

a mass synchronous cellular orgasm
or a mid-autumn so golden it entered
the blood or a day where nobody died

or those mornings when I wake up
before you to the static of early rain
and your face is so wantless and still

and mine and you're not even being
a person and you're perfect still perfect
and I have to turn away because I can't

bear to look because there's something there writhing
in you that if considered for more than a pulse would open
me up it would open me up then undo me

Current events

I'm not saying I'd never get bloody.
I would. For money, or respect,
or for a dwindling population
of bumblebees and their yellow socks,
but I'm no soldier for love.
You can't expect the flayed to go out
and continue flaying—like, ask the slug
to meet you on the other end
of the salt mine and you get no more slug.
I need the bundle
of it shoved into my hands at the entrance
of the station like the paper, one
where every headline is *I want you.*
Letter to the editor: *do you think*
it'll always feel this good? and the editor
says *oh god yes.*
An anti-muse. Stop making. Take me
in. Want me how a sentence wants
an end, how a memory wants to be
spoken. With the urgency of breath
when the bag is finally removed
from the head.

Perspective

1.

If you didn't already know I'm sorry
you have to find out this way (poem) but
everyone has very small mites living
on their eyelashes,
harmless needle-head arachnids
who eat from your pores
and mate in the full moon
of your pupil, their little lives
indebted to a big
god on which they depend
but can't understand.

2.

Before you're awake
I toss yesterday's pizza boxes,
headbutt the neighbor's cat.
Slow morning. You dig in soil.
I argue with you about snails
(let them live!)
and you put your hand up my skirt.
Again it becomes night
or what looks like night. Another
new feeling is invented. We
sleep. Sometimes I do feel
like I'm being watched. We're here,
and that's enough, but what aren't we
seeing? Hey baby, you and me,
what miracle do we serve?

2.

'It's me or the dog,' she laughed,
though by 'dog' she meant 'void'
and by 'laughed' I mean 'sobbed'
and by 'me' she meant 'us'
and by 'she' I mean 'you'
and by 'or' she meant 'and.'
'It's us and the void,' you sobbed.

Caroline Bird

We will give each other a disease to which we alone are the
cure, the curse that reinfects, the reinfection that's the cure.

Luke Kennard

Pigeon poem

It's like, if your day's
ruined over every one-footed
pigeon tripping through Liverpool Street
in search of a half-eaten fry
then it's time to leave the planet
lest you learn about the rest.
Still it's upsetting to see. A tumorous
head. A backwards wing. A body flat
as bad news.
I saw one once on its back, alive
but dying. It blinked at me
like a haunted puppet
from the hearse of the curb.
I should have stepped on its brain
but skin remembers. So do I.
You'll get by now that
all this is sad because pigeons
do know how to hurt
but don't know how to sin,
this is why I'm not quite
so sad about me,
I get exactly what I deserve.

Nightmare stations

after Rhiannon McGavin

other people's dreams are not
interesting they're like the story of someone else's
biblically charged LSD epiphany
or childhood VHS tape
full of insight for the titular
character and nothing at all for anyone else

but other people's nightmares

purple misfires

that's insight for us all

are you listening? this is important

baby I need you to understand what I've seen

put these on

I'm sorry I know they're cold

I know they're cold

X X X X X X X X X X X X X X X X X X X X X X X X X X X X X X X
X X X X X X X X X X X X X X X X X X X X X X X X X X X X X X X
X X X X X X X X X X X X X X X X X X X X X X X X X X X X X X X
X X X X X X X X X X X X X X X X X X X X X X X X X X X X X X X
X X X X X X X X X X X X X X X X X X X X X X X X X X X X X X X
X X X X X X X X X X X X X X X X X X X X X X X X X X X X X X X
X X X X X X X X X X X X X X X X X X X X X X X X X X X X X X X
X X X X X X X X X X X X X X X X X X X X X X X X X X X X X X X
X X X X X X X X X X X X X X X X X X X X X X X X X X X X X X X
X X X X X X X X X X X X X X X X X X X X X X X X X X X X X X X
X X X X X X X X X X X X X X X X X X X X X X X X X X X X X X X
X X X X X X X X X X X X X X X X X X X X X X X X X X X X X X X
X X X X X X would you take your date to the X X X X X X X X X X
X X X X X X X X X X X X X X X X X X X X X X X X X X X X X X X
X X X X X X X X X X X X X X X X X X X X X X X X X X X X X X X
X X X X X X X X X X X X X X X X X X X X X X X X X X X X X X X
X X X X X X X X X X X X X X X X X X X X X X X X X X X X X X X
X X X X X X X X X X X X X X X X X X X X X X X X X X X X X X X
X X X X X X X X X X X X X X X X X X X X X X X X X X X X X X X
X X X X X X X X X X X X X X X X X nerve center X X X X X X X X
X X X X X X X X X X X X X X X X X X X X X X X X X X X X X X X
X X X X X X X X X X X X X X X X X X X X X X X X X X X X X X X
X X X X X X X X X X X X X X X X X X X X X X X X X X X X X X X
X X X X X X X X X X X X X X X X X X X X X X X X X X X X X X X
X X X X X X X X X X X X X X X X X X X X X X X X X X X X X X X
X X X X lovers' noise was what they called X X X X X X X X X X
X X X X X X X X X X X X X X X X X X X X X X X X X X X X X X X
X X X X X X X X X X X X X X X X X X X X X X X X X X X X X X X
X X X X X X X X X X X X X X X X X X X X X X X X X X X X X X X
X X X X X X X X X X X X X X X X X X X X X X X X X X X X X X X
X X X X X X X X X X X X X X X X X X X X X X X X X X X X X X X
X X X X X X X X X X X X X X X X X X X X X X X X X X X X X X X
X X X X X X X X X X X X X X X X X X X X X X X X X X X X X X X
X X X X X X X X X X X X X X X X X X X X X X X X X X X X X X X
X X X X X X X X X X X X X X X X X X X X X X X X X X X X X X X
X X X X X X X X X X X X X X X X X X X X X X X X X X X X X X X
X X X X X X X X X X X X X X X X X X X X X X X X X X X X X X X
X X X X X X X X X X X X X X X X X X X X X X X X X X X X X X X
X X X X X X X X X X X X X X X X X X X X X X X X X X X X X X X
X X X X X X X X X X X X X X X X X X X X X X the awful sound X X X
X X X X X X X X X X X X X X X X X X X X X X X X X X X X X X X
X X X X X X X X X X X X X X X X X X X X X X X X X X X X X X X
X X X X X X X X X X X X X X X X X X X X X X X X X X X X X X X
X [a pinging, like the band of your brain has snapped] X X X X X

001.

> navigating # our great stonemetal city
> after years # of shouldering past
> sitting ducks # on escalators # I know
> every cranny # but somehow found myself
> lost en route to you!!!! >>>

> every line was black # frayed as a spider ran
> twice through a shredder # + the stations
> had no names or wrong ones >>>> Slack Jaw #
> Rearward # Up-Top >>>> I was SO late # when
> I'd finally slunk # to the end of the moving
> tube # chromatic # buskers singing
> in hostile languages
> I accosted
> a backward carriage with my fists # and
> the power of my mind # pried open the doors # sat
> almost immediately # my knees knocked knees

                    [[Hello. # Stranger.]]

> the stranger asked without words what I'd done
> to deserve # such a sunny morning
> then the carriage thinned # was only getting thinner
> forced through the tunnel's eyelet # like invasive
> cells
> baby # I don't know how
> I'll ever get back to you # since we'll be here
> forever
> the stranger looked deeper # into the darkness
> and said *I think we came from this*
> *direction*

002.

> do you remember when we # were the puppets
> gloved by the darkness # it smelled
> like my first boyfriend in that haunted
> house....
> I wanted to leave for obvious reasons

> When we kissed # our shapes came to the wall
> house-sized shadows # I moved my lips
> from you but the giant inky me didn't follow
> I sensed my own not-eyes had opened
> to look at us # even in the monochrome
> pool of its face

> I know how it sounds but
> the world is getting stranger and stranger
> and we can't rule anything out......

> me and I looked at each other for a season
> September happened # nothing changed

> I think what I saw wasn't us at all
> but some other thing that had stolen our bodies
> infinitely old # and living in the walls
> I want every line
> my life writes # to be explicable

003.

   > undoing. you refused to acknowledge me
   > when I arrived at the lake and everyone
   > we've ever drank with noticed # my tits
   > were out but that wasn't important!
   > the brown grease of it # this
   > ugliness wearing your face
   > You kissed *her* # I was right there :(>>>>

      << why is it so hard to take a fucking picture
          of the moon it never looks right >>

   > my belly felt like clam flesh # the disposable
   > viscera from which the more important
   > pearls are wrenched # Meanwhile
   > you smiled at her with your teeth. Bling bling.
   > Disgusting! I threw myself into the water
· ### (to die!) ###
   > a snake wriggled up behind me # muscle
   > desperate to keep living
   > or just to move forward # I watched
   > the moment as if through tortures
   > of kaleidoscopes # a bigger snake moved

```
           > to its tail and unhinged
           > its mouth and began to # eat,
           > a river consumed by a hungrier # mightier river
  Ha-ha!   > I laughed, and thought that
           > since the threat came from behind
           > and in the same shape #
           > it won't even know it's being devoured
           > until it's too late # # # # # # #
```

004.

> oh my shared humanity # I knew from
> the second it hit
> water # that the flayed red astronaut
> the size of a fist
> was ours >>>>
> I'll admit that I'm horrified # of my own
> biology
          ** Its limits   Its failures
> What it craves # A chain link # organ

> Little vessel circled like a ship
> made of flesh # going nowhere >>>>>>

> it was my fault for only wanting a child
> so it could warn us if ghosts were nearby
> that's very very very selfish

                    [[We could .
            have one day taught it the right way [
            to pet an animal   ] [the direction
                    the hair grows]
            X X X X that there are people here
              photographing black holes X X X X
            there are people here who will want badly
            to touch your wrists # until you shiver]]

> Botched consciousness #
> wearing our average eyes # that inverted
> expression # I knew it >>>>>>>

```
> My body can't make life # or love #
> Just mistakes

> I feel we cannot survive this
                    . . . . . . .
                     . . . .
                      . .
```

005.

> hello # HELLO
> listen if you can hear me from where you are
> you and I fucked in the middle
> of a wide American road
> while every natural disaster at once
> around us hacked # its lungs
> sideways!!!!!!
> telephone poles collapsed # and spat orange
> sparks!!!!!!
> a car no one was driving # whooshed
> by # an AMBER alert pulsed from its radio
                [[[EVERYONE IS MISSING]]]
> I don't know why # when the lightning
> struck your back and opened
> you # I couldn't feel the pain
> of the current # only your usual chest # pressed
> against my chest #
> your dead weight

006.

EVERYONE IN THE WORLD CAN HEAR <
HOW I AM EMBARRASSING MYSELF <
ON THE STAIRS # ok I know your friends think <
I'm crazy # limp-wristed no-fight <
like swinging fists at # an unspidered web <

you hated me <
how a moth hates the dark # which <
is not hatred # as in indifference <
as in the more tantalizing # brightness <
of every other possible thing <

you told me how good she was to hold <
+ how you held her # like a view in an eye <

[[a boring weather report <
rain again in London infant brain <
you should have known]] <

I turned away from you so quickly <
I entered a new timeline <

...followed you up to your room <
with the wrong view <
the new fire escape # train hovering a finger's <
width above the tracks # your same house <
but made from a coalition of small evil spaces <
licking their lips <
looking at me without # eyes <

and I couldn't help myself <
[little solar systems <
populated only # by anti-natalists <
all of them hemorrhaging] <

<< do you find me the push # or the pull??? >>

pinned you to the bed <
even when I struck you <
you wouldn't look at me <
what have you done <
your head rolled <
from the fungal stalk of your neck <
a bag of sand on a tree branch <
your tongue # bloated <

you were so elsewhere <
I don't even think you realized <
what was happening <

how could you ruin us <

your jaw lengthened # your features <
drifted outwards <

I wretched <
something black <

My singular sweetness I could never hate you <
                            I hate your power <
                     I hate your hurting hands <

007.

every night at least a morsel of love
lies in bed with at least a morsel of power
and if you disagree
you either have so much or so little
you can't even see it's there
(like water like life)

. . . _ _ _ . . .

```
X X X X X X X X X X X X X X X X X X X X X X X X X X X X X X X X X X X X X X X X
X X X X X X X X X X X X X X X X X X X X X X X X X X X X X X X X X X X X X X X X
X X X X X X X X X X X X X X X X X X X X X X X X X X X X X X X X X X X X X X X X
X X X X X X X X X X X X X X X X X X X X X X X X X X X X X X X X X X X X X X X X
X X X X X X X X X X X X X X X X X X X X X X X X X X X X X X X X X X X X X X X X
X X X X X X X X X X X X X X X X X X X X X X X X X X X X X X X X X X X X X X X X
X X X X X X X X X X X X X X X X X X X X X X X X X X X X X X X X X X X X X X X X
X X X X X X X X X X X X X X X X X X X X X X X X X X X X X X X X X X X X X X X X
X X X X X X X X X X X X X X X X X X X X X X X X X X X X X X X X X X X X X X X X
X X X X X X X X X X X X X X X X X X X X X X X X X X X X X X X X X X X X X X X X
X X X X X X X X X X X X X X X X X X X X X X X X X X X X X X X X X X X X X X X X
X X X X X X X X X X X X X X X X X X X X X X X X X X X X X X X X X X X X X X X X
X X X X X X X X X X X X X X X X X X X X X X X X X X X X X X X X X X X X X X X X
X X X X X X X X X X X X X X X X X X X X X X X X X X X X X X X X X X X X X X X X
X X X X X X X X X X X X X X X X X X X X X X X X X X X X X X X X X X X X X X X X
X X X X X X X X X X X X X X X X X X X X X X X X X X X X X X X X X X X X X X X X
X X X X X X X X X X X X X X X X X X X X X X X X X X X X X X X X X X X X X X X X
X X X X X X X X X X X X X X X X X X X X X X X X X X X X X X X X X X X X X X X X
X X X X X X X X X X X X X X X X X X X X X X X X X X X X X X X X X X X X X X X X
X X X X X X X X X X X X X X X X X X X X X X X X X X X X X X X X X X X X X X X X
X X X X X X X X X X X X X X X X X X X X X X X X X X X X X X X X X X X X X X X X
X X X X X X X X X X X X X X X X X X X X X X X X X X X X X X X X X X X X X X X X
X X X X X X X X X X X X X X X X X X X X X X X X X X X X X X X X X X X X X X X X
X X X X X X X X X X X X X X X X X X X X X X X X X X X X X X X X X X X X X X X X
X X X X X X X X X X X X X X X X X X X X X X X X X X X X X X X X X X X X X X X X
X X X X X X X X X X X X X X X X X X X X X X X X X X X X X X X X X X X X X X X X
X X X X X X X X X X X X X X X X X X X X X X X X X X X X X X X X X X X X X X X X
X X X X X X X X X X X X X X X X X X X X X X X X X X X X X X X X X X X X X X X X
X X X X X X X X X X X X X X X X X X X X X X X X X X X X X X X X X X X X X X X X
X X X X X X X X X X X X X X X X X X X X X X X X X X X X X X X X X X X X X X X X
X X X X X X X X X X X X X X X X X X X X X X X X X X X X X X X X X X X X X X X X
X X X X X X X X X X X X X X X X X X X X X X X X X X X X X X X X X X X X X X X X
X X X X X X X X X X X X X X X X X X X X X X X X X X X X X X X X X X X X X X X X
X X X X X X X X X X X X X X X X X X X X X X X X X X X X X X X X X X X X X X X X
X X X X X X X X what makes you so fucking X X X X X X X X X X X X
X X X X X X X X X X X X X X X X X X X X X X X X X X X X X X X X X X X X X X X X
X X X X X X X X X X X X special X X X X X X X X X X X X X X X X X X X X X
X X X X X X X X X X X X X X X X X X X X X X X X X X X X X X X X X X X X X X X X
X X X X X X X X X X X X X X X X X X X X X X X X X X X X X X X X X X X X X X X X
X X X X X X X X X X X X X X X X X X X X X X X X X X X X X X X X X X X X X X X X
X X X X X X X X X X X X X X X X X X X X X X X X X X X X X X X X X X X X X X X X
X X X X X X X X X X X X X X X X X X X X X X X X X X X X X X X X X X X X X X X X
```

The day of the flying ants

On the bench we speak
about what it would look like
to end things. Before this
the flying ants came out to fuck
then die. I'm asking for answers.
I'm asking for therapy when she lands
on my lap and thinks about
nothing then chews her wings
from her body and walks on.
She was made
for this. This act is part of her
design. The time is now. Wing
meet tongue. Meet
teeth. Look at me.
I can walk
anywhere you're not.

3.

Do not cease dancing, you lovely girls!

Friedrich Nietzsche

Wilhelm yawp

start with the oeuvre   no the needy texts   no just
you in the back of a taxicab supple and sparkling
here you are   poured into your clothes   and wow!
you look great   go get 'em champ   so many liquids
and pink little pills!   you try to be tender
at least once per day   you have a dangerous
complex   a miserable birthday   you know it's not
about when you arrive but how long you stay   smell
rain-loosened earth and suspect this phenomenon
should be given a name   you go to the night club
and   the   theme   is   the   human   experience
choose then to be tender and   uh oh bad timing
but   your skin looks killer   think satin miniskirts
only for this miracle   you consider the multiverse
and   make poor decisions   not in that order   make
friends who talk to small non-human animals
as if they're children   make sure all your friends
are gods   you want to be loved religiously
and   learn to knot a ribbon of light with only
your tongue and teeth   climb two hundred
stairs in the cold to pretend you are the height
from which the water falls   watch the peak
terns curl like possessive apostrophes   fall asleep
in a clover field   you synthesize elegies   bashfully
refuse an effigy   you become the great sound
that wraps round the moon   you articulate madman
you void-sucking poet you! you! you! are so afraid
that in the middle of your breakup fuck this life
will moan to no confusion some other baby's name

Shared consciousness of the party girl

When you need me look up
from your shoes on any busy street past
setting hour, I'm there,

a neon-blush exclamation
mark glitching through the dark
looking to attach herself

to anything for emphasis.
In the city it's easy to feel like
you're doing something

important but this cupid's bow says
I actually am. I've come in search of the very best
nighttime and I'm ready to confess

I'd like some attention.
I know you want it too, a bed full of people
who all want to touch you first,

immortality
can be achieved by having poison drawn
from your belly button

by a stranger in interesting eyeliner,
I know nothing about flesh, know none
of what it knows but is trying

so hard to tell me,
it's a language like birdsong sung
in reverse, something beautiful and wrong,

a moment feeling nostalgic for itself,
a big gun, a little knife,
the plush of a belly turned up, expectant,

take all of us home honey,
we'll show you the things we can do.

My god, girlhood ripened

like roadkill in the sun Even if
we were for our glorious
seventeenth earth year the subject
of all of those songs One teenage
dream rises from the dead
to find her sepulcher full of chirping
webcams Another streaks across sites
bent on the protection of her just-
-erected loneliness No one
tells the goody-two-shoes to take
the pot smoke all the way into
her gore
So while the nobleboys cackle,
atlas psychedelic labyrinths
    She's just soberly walking through
           the family planning aisle
Fine that one was me I'm a little bitter
But you know they're all me
Did all of us not let our virgin
boyfriend's tongue expire
in our mouths like an invasive
species of fish Did he not drive
us all home long before curfew

Did a cyberspace-based taxpayer
not make us all his baby muse
A bouquet
of electric toothbrushes shivering
in the nightstand gives you away
and The birthday girl is finally
allowed to look
in the mirror
        Now I'm older
so the sort of young that knows
things Like hurting someone first feels
like flying And only people
who don't write die   Just grin and bear
it suburb sugar we'll get you
outta there Oh I only want to write
about tomorrow Tomorrow
I'll be wiser and scarier
and so much harder to trick oh
it will be the best
and only day of my life

Call and response

(I used to think
the sexiest thing a woman
could do was answer

to any name   Now
I know it's the silence   The
never answering

What girlish secrets
could she be hiding
in the absence of sound)

THE HOTTEST GIRL IN THE WORLD!!!!!

is drinking gallons and gallons
    of oat milk
and has completely undetectable scoliosis

She is wearing low-cut
    paradoxes and thinks about her boyfriend
for a minimum
    of nine hours an earth day

When she lifts her arms to stretch
    her spine she reveals a belly button
    shaped like a coin slot
to a vending machine that dispenses
goodtime

She is vividly sexy and precious and dying
like the coral reef as photographed for Playboy

She is moving to a city near you
    She is online now and ready to chat

We know
where she lives

She *is* gorilla grip
  She *is* scarce resource

She is coquettishly pulling your terrible
   pint and her tweets do not suck

We would kill
                      (ourselves for) her

She's just passed the bar exam and
      we're so very proud

She met your parents before you were born
      and it went really well

Her many kinks include
  being tied up and then let go
    over and over and

      she is coming just for you

Look she is creating an OnlyFans to which everyone alive
will   subscribe

Breaking news
in a small town in Nowhere
   the new world's hottest girl was just born
      and we have exclusive images of her delivery

Meanwhile we have decided to crucify the old one

We are crucifying her in New York and in London
We are crucifying her on the cover of The Times
On TMZ she is being asked what it feels like to hang
there

Understand there is nothing more important than the world's
hottest girl

Our glittery idiot savior
The exquisite god we despise

What sounds like a girl laughing

Revelations flit through the city like loose glitter scraped
from a false star. The dream boat from Venus I've met
just tonight keeps calling me *the masochist's daughter*, God
I want her. I am trying so hard to not watch her piss
in this basement stall of New Cross Inn. At some point
the nighttime girls all went to a class called 'how to comfortably
 piss in front of the others' and I did not go. They also
went to a class called 'how to arrive all at once and then sizzle
out of existence like a snowball tossed at a windowpane'.
My hands are full of wanting something to hold.
Biblemen too witnessed archangels and all their thousand eyes,
and astronauts witness the black pool yawning
underneath the Earth, what is everything except us and the sky,
what sounds to some like a girl laughing, laughing all the way down.

Seduction theory

Once I made out with a pair of twins in one night
so let it be known when I want something I want more
of it than usually exists. Everyone at the party follows
me into the other room like a group of anthropologists
trying to solve an ancient mystery. My back became
a swollen star map to nowhere after fucking in the woods.
Every drug makes me want my hair stroked and you would
not believe all the places you can be emotionally volatile in.
My boyfriends have been congratulated. I've worn still lakes
as thigh highs. Someday I will conduct an uncomplicated orgy
where everyone knows exactly what to do with their hands.
I've filled journals with fantasies about people who hate me,
imprisoned people in my mind, and they're still there.
Feeling something that is almost pain. Their aliveness
is dazzling with what is almost purpose.

Animal, impulse

Like all good friends she speaks of sex and fear simply
as bad governments. The mind confuses one for
the other. A Möbius strip of craving, getting; sooner or
later you'll find yourself [...] completely unravelled,
having forgotten your name, what new world you hoped for
when you agreed to this self-possession. Fine. Control
is the filthy miracle we're all better off without.

Jeff Bezos' sexts

(part 2 of this poem was written only using words and phrases from the leaked
texts Jeff Bezos sent to his then-mistress Lauren Sanchez in 2019)

1.

I enjoy those quick thought experiments
meant to demonstrate the immense
distance between *million* and *billion*
so I've come up with a new one and here it is
let's say the average female orgasm
lasts for twenty seconds therefore
one could have three orgasms a minute
therefore one could have 4,320 orgasms
a day therefore it would take 231 and a half
days to have one million orgasms

which of course would be........intense
and might damage you........irreparably
I don't know what happens to the body
I don't know what happens to the mind
I'm not sure if you could move on
from that

but to have one billion orgasms
you would need to be orgasming for 634 years
which is longer than America has existed
longer than the good bits of Rome
can you imagine being a medieval peasant
and having the weirdest thing ever happen to you
only catch your breath and hear some magic
glass say a man has landed on the moon

though it's probably a more positive
or enjoyable way to be a person
than some people
have tried

2.

Yesterday 06:49

My alive girl
I woke up with a tight feeling
Had coffee, read the paper
I think I'll not be quite so gentle tomorrow

Yesterday 06:50

You have to WANT it alive girl
You have to fall asleep and wake up wanting it

Yesterday 06:55

and I WANT TO BE WITH YOU!!!

Yesterday 10:34

I mean I want to get know you
Like I know the room of my heart
when it's swollen to the size of the body

Yesterday 16:13

Alive girl you were made to better me
YOU were made to turn me on

Yesterday 21:12

Tucked into bed I'm thinking of
your sleepy little laugh
the smell of fall
lips kissed gently, with drunk competence

Yesterday 21:30

not falling down drunk
just a little drunk

Yesterday 21:49

I'm in love with you alive girl
I will show you with my ideas
With my wanting

Yesterday 22:11

Did you plan for this?

Yesterday 22:55

Basically I have to have you with the little
The little
The very very little
I have

Yesterday 23:14

And what is bigger than the heart?

Today 00:12

Alive girl
Tell me

Today 00:15

Alive girl show me
your gentle spirit

Today 01:55

It's up to you not to breathe

Today 02:22

. love ! . ! . . ! . love . show . . . love ? . . . love . . .

3.

Today 15:21

ok

Every time we go on a walk we're like wow look at that house

I think of the us we'd become in a beam of luxurious light.
I want the dregs of this world suctioned out of my home
through a very expensive tube. Everyone on the news is an actor
I've hired by the sheer power of my good fortune. I only breathe
gold-spangled particles. Around us the times are inflating.
What wonderful material money is made from, so slippery
and clean, covered in the faces of men. I'll slurp every drop.
I   will   have   a   glorious   gem-studded   wingspan
with which I will not be able to touch either side of my kitchen.
If I fall I will be caught. When I die my commemorative plaque
will be bluer than new water. My friends rent the rooms
of people who hate them. I want my piece. I want something
unlosable. I know you're worried. My friends are making money
for people who hate them. I did not make a profit today
so will not tell many jokes. My friends have lost their money
in cryptocurrency. I would love to be able to pass down
to my children a plot in which things are able to grow.
I will earn a blue plaque but it will not suit the landlady's
façade. You know most stained glass these days is just a sticker.
You can tell by its geometry, how it doesn't hold the light in its
belly. Sunlight filtered through stained glass takes on other-
worldly properties. God I love the long shadows in the evening.
I'm sorry the drawbridge was pulled while you were away. No
I don't know the answer. I don't know the stupid answer.

Everything is very complicated

The first cell that wanted something another cell wanted
invented despair and here is something called a thirst
trap

As we speak the bare digital tits of someone you know
hurdle through cyberspace

Our brethren's dicks
are lodged in the archives of a phone
like popcorn in a tooth

Oh I've pulled him before she says casually like *pulling him* is slang
for going to an exhibition or being sad
when really she might have licked his armpit
or cried when she came
which I'm sorry are different and important things

Your betrothed's old unrequited love
attends the function and your teeth leap from your head

You think of the short stretch of time
                    where the mind outlives the body
                    and consider masturbating

The body is a coalition
of incompatible miracles

Everyone wants somebody
to understand their personality
and their childhood
and what each of those things
has done to the other one

in the pursuit of this understanding
they embarrass themselves
and break many drug laws

The past is a cryptid no one can identity
but everyone's been abducted by
and shares stories about round campfires

There's only what we've felt and speculation

Look up at the high ceiling of the heart's
atrium, this waiting room echoes
and echoes,
   everything that was ever inside stays,
your big ideas, the gossip of the rain,
the collective voice
   of everyone you've loved
asking if you're not

the self you've given away, then what

Vacation

I have looked into tide pools and found nothing
    alive
I have watched a bead of sweat drop
    onto ancient rock from the last place
        you kissed

The water sparkles here like it's possessed
    by heaven

When you're standing on a mountain it's easy to think
if you got every person into your living
room you could figure this whole thing out

You know when the rain starts
    the second you're safely inside
    and take off your shoes
Both watched and unwatched
Like suddenly I don't remember
who told me
I need to be so clever

Top comment

I have never had an original
experience in my life

I'd send this to my boyfriend
but you're too pretty

This world is full
of the left and the leaving

A living machine
only tries to answer hard questions
correctly

Our fear harmonized
like a grade school choir
trying, and full of tomorrows

Once on vacation I watched
more than a thousand people gather round a pier
to take the exact same picture of the sun

I'm sure this breeze is related
to the force that invented consciousness

Would you ever want to find out
how many miracles you have left
or do you want it to be a surprise

Everyone wants to know
if it ever snowed in the town you grew up in

The thought of getting a drink with my mom
when she was the age I am now
makes me cry

In my childhood home small pieces
of skin float in the air and catch
light rays like human confetti

My friends I'll use my intelligence
to love you better

Young geniuses
Accidental astronauts
I'll get to the place where you are

Notes + acknowledgements

Thank you to the editors of the publications in which these poems appeared previously: 'Wilhelm yawp' in *World-Dreem* and 'THE HOTTEST GIRL IN THE WORLD!!!!!' in *Violet Indigo Blue, Etc.*

'Animal, impulses' is an aye, a form invented by poet Ian Macartney characterized by six twelve-syllable lines that include a 'quantum jump' ([...]). Ian is also a good friend but that has nothing to do with it.

Olbers' paradox is the problem of why an infinitely large universe isn't bright with infinite stars.

The title of 'Wilhelm yawp' references a combination of the Wilhelm scream (the stock audio of a man's scream used so commonly in film and TV that it became infamous) and Walt Whitman's 'barbaric yawp'. I liked the idea of a yawp so common it became a joke, thus, title. Many people told me to change it.

It's important to me that you know that I didn't invent the phrase 'my alive girl' in 'Jeff Bezos' sexts'; he said that.

Thank you to Mark Radley, Richard Pike, Claire Maxwell and Daniel Lisi. Thank you Rhiannon McGavin for being a wonderful editor and friend. Thanks to Zoe Norvell for the cover design. Thanks to Kitty, Connie, Maja, Bert and Mom + Dad, always. Ewan: I've no idea what will happen. What fun, what fun.

Savannah Brown is an American writer living in London. *Closer Baby Closer* is her fifth book. You can find her at @savannahbrown on Twitter and @savbrown on Instagram.